A Morning Routine

More Energetic, Productive, Stress-Free Days for Those of Us With Normal Lives

Lola R. Marie

Authors Note: Sign-up for a free Sleep Chart to aid in your mission of creating better mornings. You can download the Sleep Chart at www.lolarmarie.com/sign-up

Part 1

Introduction

When I set out to write this book, I knew I had to make some changes to my lifestyle. Having followed a morning routine for over a year now and having watched it guide me to where I stand today, I was well aware of its incredible benefits. I wanted to share my experience with everyone who could benefit from it. In particular, I wanted to share it with those, who like me, had set schedules that demanded their time and presence. We hear about this celebrity or that vlogger and their life-changing morning routine. How they effortlessly glide out of bed onto their balcony to watch a sunrise with a warm cup of coffee. They read for an hour, water their plants and head to the gym. Initially I thought, "Great, but how do I do that? I have a normal job!" However, with some research, a bit of experimentation and a dash of realism, I found something that worked. I wanted to let people know that despite their busy lifestyles and pre-determined schedules, they could, like me, find time and in the process re-discover themselves by incorporating an effective morning routine.

It worked like magic for me and I am convinced beyond a doubt that it will work for anyone who wants to attempt it. And so, in my quest to make this book as authentic and versatile as it can be, I began practicing different morning routines for fixed periods (enough time for me to validate their results). To begin with, I woke up at 5.am every day during the course of researching and writing this book. I wanted to experience how and what I felt and the results were outstanding. This book is a direct result of that enriching experience.

I learned how simple adaptation, such as waking up a little ahead of my usual time and making a routine out of it, prepared me to face the future. I felt more energetic, productive, and purposeful. I began to feel more sorted and at peace with myself. And that feeling has only grown with each passing morning. Adapting to a morning routine that works for me has made a profound effect on my life. It has, by all means, changed the trajectory of my otherwise hectic and time-starved life.

You see, I too struggled with time and felt rushed until a year ago. Mornings were a chaotic time for me. I spent years struggling to cope with the haze. I always felt short-changed for time and I always tried to speed things up without actually giving the work the time it needed. Needless to say, I felt so drained and defeated by the end of the day that any drive to undertake a side-hustle or passion project in the evening would be squashed even before I allowed the thought to enter my mind. Everyday fed into a negative cycle of living a repetitive dreary lifestyle. I was full of hope and ideas, yet I felt stuck which fostered a subconscious form of resentment.

I've been there and know exactly how it feels. However, I've also finally moved over from that phase and into a more productive and fulfilling one. And that is why writing this book is so important to me.

Why Have a Morning Routine

The way we spend our mornings has a profound effect on the rest of our day. In essence, mornings hold the key to taking control of our calendars, and in due course, our lives too. It is the choices we make during the first few hours of our day that determine how productive and content we feel by night.

As part of my research for this book, I've met up with dozens of individuals and poured through journals of extremely successful people so as to understand what they believe is the key to their everlasting happiness (or success as some people would like to call it). And the one thing that stood out, the single most common habit, was that they all believed there was a better way to start the day than rushing through it. They all swore by their morning routine and never left their mornings to chance.

Sure, they all had different routines, each built to suit their needs and lifestyles, but that's the beauty of it. Morning routines aren't about blindly following a single set of rules that works for all. Because frankly speaking, they don't. Some routines might require you to be an early riser; others might be more luxurious and self-indulgent. In the end, it's all about helping you find a routine that allows you to be your most productive and happy self, and I'm here to guide you through every step of that journey.

From introducing you to sleep patterns to encouraging you make health and lifestyle alterations, this book will give you a wide range of possible practices to explore and master, all at the convenience of your time and choice of place.

How to Read This Book

Throughout this book, you'll find excerpts from conversations I've had with highly successful people. These people aren't celebrities, nor are they famous (we have plenty of books on that already). But, they are equally talented and hardworking. They, much like you and I, started out with modest beginnings. They mostly have "normal" jobs that expect them to be at a certain place and at a certain time. They have families and responsibilities that they are accountable for. They are happy, successful and do a darn good job in each of their roles, which is why they make for perfect role models.

If you have a job that demands your presence at a certain place and at a certain time, then this book is for you. Likewise, if you are a student who has got heaps of study material to pour through or have a family that needs your presence and could do with a few more hours in a day, then this book is for you. This book is especially written with all of you in mind.

The point I'm trying to make with this book is that there isn't a single bullet-proof morning routine that works. There needn't be one too. I understand that we are all different people and therefore have different needs. And so, I've made this book very practical. We all don't desire to become multi-millionaires, secure a demanding fast-paced career or live a nomadic lifestyle. In my opinion, success isn't measured by what and how much we've accomplished, but an internal sense of peace no matter the external situation.

The first part of the book consists of reading and referenced material, practical solutions, tips and the second part includes meditation scripts (which are also available in audio format) for you to pick and explore.

I ask of you to read this book with an open mind, even stopping to take notes or reflect on something that intrigues you. I want you to explore and improvise on different routines until you've formed a morning routine that works for you: one that makes you feel alive, happy and at peace. Think of your mornings as a blank slate. You now have the opportunity to fill it with whatever you want and start again.

Remember that it's the little things we do every day that have the power to impact our lives and shape our dreams. And having a morning routine that works can be your first step in scripting that dream.

Go Live Your Dream
Lola

Chapter 1 - The Act of Waking-Up

In a world that's quick to assume and even more quick to judge, a lot of attention is given to validating how productive and useful a person is. Sadly, everything is put down to how many hours you work, what numbers you bring in, and by that math, what you are worth.

Sure, waking up in the morning and having morning routines set in place are great ways to begin the day and achieve those numbers (as well as everything else you seek from life). But because rest directly influences whether or not you're likely to stay on a morning routine and because your body requires rest to replenish and thrive, it is very important that we discuss...

THIS THING CALLED SLEEP, before we discuss about mornings and morning routines. After all, sleep is the best form of rest your body can get.

As Charlotte Bronte fittingly put it, "A ruffled mind makes a restless pillow." Getting a good 7-9 hours of sleep every night (and I say night only because it's innately how our biological clock works) can do wonders to your body as well as your mornings. On the contrary, sleep disruption is the most common contributor to chronic illnesses and major psychiatric conditions, including heart disease, high blood pressure, diabetes, depression, anxiety, and suicidal thoughts (none of which we want to inherit).

Why and How We Sleep

It turns out that the practice of sleep did not happen merely by human evolution or chance. On the contrary, the process of "sleep" has been so deep-set into our biological systems that left by itself, our bodies need little thought or effort to go into this state. It is as natural as you breathe and live. It therefore needs a lot of self-destructive practices to disrupt this natural phenomenon. Sadly, self-destruction can sometimes be a common human trait with the added help of the man-made systems in place.

Sleep is a complex set of metabolic activities that induces energy-releasing and life-replenishing benefits to your body. For one, the functions of your brain are restored and revived as you sleep. Good sleep can catapult your ability to calibrate, learn, memorize, and decide. It regulates emotional brain health, thus allowing us to go through social and psychological tasks with logical rationale. In essence, sleep writes out a hoard of health-ensuring benefits, yours to collect in repeat prescription every day, should you choose. Many don't.

Adequate sleep regulates the immune system as well as every organ in the body so as to help an individual function at his/her optimal best. It restores the body's metabolic activity just as it controls the cardiovascular system. Simply put, we sleep because we have to.

Stages of Sleep

Sleep is determined by two stages: rapid eye movement (REM) sleep and non-REM sleep (which is spaced across three different stages). Each stage triggers precise brain waves and neuronal activity as they coincide in a recurring and almost push-pull battle for brain supremacy during the duration of sleep. That said, although you toggle back and forth between the two stages several times during sleep, you are more inclined to drift towards longer and deeper periods of REM sleep towards the morning.

Stage 1 non-REM sleep is when you shift from a state of wakefulness to sleep. During this phase (and it can last for several minutes), your body subconsciously prepares itself in anticipation of the rest it is likely to get. Your heartbeat, breathing, and eye movements slow down while coaxing your muscles to relax. Your brainwaves too slow down so as to prepare for rest.

Stage 2 non-REM sleep is the next phase of sleep and precedes deeper sleep. It is the intermediate period of sleep so to speak. While your heartbeat and breathing remain low, your muscles ease even further. Body temperature decreases and eyes make minimal movement. Brain wave activity too slows down considerably, however, it is triggered by random sessions of electrical activity.

Stage 3 non-REM sleep is the period of deep sleep that you need to feel fresh in the morning and tends to stretch out during the first half of the night. Your heartbeat and breathing slow to their lowest levels during this phase. Muscle movement and brain wave activity are at a bare minimum during this phase.

The next phase is the REM sleep phase. You move into this phase after a little over an hour of sleep. During this phase, your eyes move briskly from side to side behind closed eyelids, marking the first signs of wakefulness. Brain wave activity gradually increases. You breathe faster as your heart rate and blood pressure increase to near waking levels. Most dreaming occurs in this phase. Muscle movement is almost completely restricted which is why it is difficult to act out one's dream.

"What is your morning routine?
I typically wake between 5:00 and 6:30 A.M. I like starting my day with some activity and so I try and do the planks for a few minutes right after I get out of bed. Then, I grab a glass of water and catch up on some reads. I give myself 20 minutes to do this. Then it's time for the kids to wake up so I make sure I am free and spend quality time with them while they get ready to go to school.

Do you do anything before bed to make your morning easier?
I take a shower at night. I've been doing this for many years and it always saves me plenty of time in the morning. Also, showering at night makes me feel relaxed. My muscles feel relaxed and I'm able to go to sleep sooner. So it all comes together."- Todd Freeman, Fire fighter

Your Body as It Awakens

As the sun courses its way closer to the horizon, the sky is filled with lighter hues. Your retina, which is located at the back of your eyes are exposed to light rays. Exposure to light stimulates neuropathways and your brain sends out signals through brainwaves to prepare for wakefulness. And as it does, your entire body and mind go through a series of complex changes (again) as it prepares to wake up. Your heart rate increases. So does your breathing and blood circulation. Your eyes open and shut and you become more sensitive to external stimuli. Liver, kidney, digestion, and metabolic functions jog back to wakeful levels.

Melatonin, a hormone with anti-cancer properties is produced in the pineal gland to regulate wakefulness. It peaks during the sleep phase, when the retina is not exposed to light. Melatonin levels lower as exposure to light increases, thus initiating the process of waking up. As you wake, the stress hormone cortisol too is on the rise. Your body temperature is at its lowest during sleep, however in the morning, it prepares to peak up to its wakeful levels.

Sleep, Wakefulness, and Their Transition into New Energy

We are all from the same star dust. And so, by birth, we are also multidimensional beings, living holograms so to speak. While we mostly function in the third and perhaps occasionally in the fourth dimensions (where restricted psychic experiences and vivid dreams take place), we all have with us the opportunity to awaken our higher self and move into higher vibrational fields, states of inner peace.

We are connected by a single thread of omnipresent and powerful energy, some call it the universe, God or source. While we all have the ability to connect to our source of powerful energy, only a few actually make a conscious connection in this lifetime. However, sleep is our door to doing just that. And the time just before you wake up (whether intentionally or not) is when you, as a physical being attempt to connect with your higher consciousness. It can be your door to spiritual awakening.

Every night, during sleep, your body prepares to connect to its higher self. It inherently attempts to evolve so as to be able to experience the dimensions beyond the 4th where all possibilities lie. And therefore, getting good sleep is crucial. Guess what will happen if you don't plug in your phone to charge? It will eventually die. Likewise, every night you recharge. You plug yourself into the life force that pervades all and recharge for the day that lies ahead. Not only does sleep give you a chance to realize your true self (and that by itself is such a profound possibility), but it also prepares your body for the possibility of profound inner growth every single night.

As discussed before, your body produces melatonin and melatonin is more than just a hormone. It is an important neurotransmitter that effects your circadian rhythm or biological clock, so as to propel it to resonate with frequencies beyond the ones known to you. By resetting your biological clock, it prepares your body for the possibility of an inner energy shift.

Our transition into higher consciousness wakes us in more ways than one. Understanding just how our physical, emotional, and metaphysical components come together during sleep for a single purpose (to connect us with our source), can help us realize our self and in that process realize our life's purpose.

Chapter 2 - Benefits of a Morning Routine

"How do you start your day?

Well, I start it the previous night actually. I need my sleep or I feel washed out for the rest of the next day. So, I make sure I stay active and exhaust my energy by night. Depending on how I feel at night and when I sleep, I try and set an alarm for anywhere between 6:30 and 7:00 A.M. Next, I make coffee, grab a book, a protein bar and tuck into my favourite corner at home. I feel the 20 minutes I get for myself during the morning helps me feel good; less rushed, and stay more productive during the day."- Jenifer Rodd – IT Professional

Like many, waking up in the morning was at the very top of my list of least favourite things to do until a year ago. If the world is made up of night owls and larks, I most definitely saw myself in the former category. But that was a while ago. A lot has changed since then, and a lot of positive outcomes have come out of it.

I wanted to work smarter and not necessarily harder. As I became more consistent with my routines, I realized how seamlessly it set the tone for the entire day. And with each morning done right, I realized how it has the potential to set my entire life right.

You see, I believe that mornings, if channelled correctly, can be the best part of your day. They can be delightful times. Times when you watch yourself shape up to the person you've always envisioned yourself to be. That experience is extremely empowering and that's putting it mildly.

You gain enormously by putting your first few hours of the day to use on projects that are most meaningful to you. When you start early on things that you've always wanted to work on, you make large strides on goals that up until then were sitting on the back burner. What's more, you carry that feeling of accomplishment for the rest of the day.

Incorporating a Physical Morning Routine Is Great Because It Makes You Feel More Physically Agile and Healthy

It's common knowledge that one must exercise, eat healthy, sleep well, and spend less time on their phones to lead a healthier life. And despite how much of this we already do, we all know that we can do a little more if we make the time for it. Spending a few additional minutes every morning on things that benefit your lifestyle can trigger a series of positive motivators. This in turn can yield positive noticeable changes.

For instance, you don't need to belt out two hours in the gym every morning to experience the benefits of a consistent exercise routine. Keeping your physical routine short and easy, will do the job. The more replicable your routine is, the more likely you are going to stick to it and this will ensure you achieve the long-term benefits you were initially after.

Truth is, physical activity in any form can do wonders to your body. Not only does it make you look your best, but it also reduces the risks of developing several diseases such as type 2 diabetes, cancer and cardiovascular diseases. Incorporating a 30-minute morning routine that keeps you physically active can:

- Reduce your risk of a heart attack
- Help you stay in your ideal weight
- Lower your blood pressure and blood cholesterol levels

- Lower the risk of type 2 diabetes and some cancers
- Leave you with stronger bones, muscles and joints and reduce your risk of developing osteoporosis
- Leave you feeling more energetic

It Can Also Make You Feel More Mentally Relaxed and At Peace

This, in my opinion, is the biggest benefit of morning routines and I can write an entire book (or two or three) on this one topic. Having had my share of "life lessons" I struggled to silence the inner chatter that constantly told me what to do and what not to do. Although, I mostly knew what the right thing to do was, it had little bearing on what I eventually found myself doing. Somehow, between my sense of realizing my goal and fulfilling it, the internal narrative always took over and executed its own plan; plans that roughly translated to procrastination over immediate action, and ignorance over acceptance. It was a form of self-sabotage I embarrassingly welcomed.

I've struggled with these issues for the longest time (and still do every now and then), but it wasn't until I found a 30-minute morning meditation routine that I was successfully able to silence the chatter and go about functioning at my best.

Through the years, I've accepted that the chatter might never fully leave. That it might come and go. It's inevitable. What is not, is that I let it affect me and break me down. Thanks to my morning routine, I've found ways to re-discover myself. I'm living my best life today and I owe it all to my morning routine. It gave birth to a whole-new-happy-and complete me.

Including a 30-minute mind morning routine that allows you to have some me-time with yourself can be a life-changing experience. I repeat and stress on this fact because that's all it takes to transform your life, it is a foundational change in which many facets can be built. You can always do more, but 30-minutes is great to get started. From personal experience, I can tell you that my mind morning routine has given me a new sense of self.

I now have more control over my thoughts, actions, and words.
I am more self-assured and less confused/conflicted
I now search for answers from within
I am my happiest and most content self.

I feel complete. And that feeling is BIG.

In essence, your morning routine can be an indicator of your present mental health, as well your disposition towards life in general. Someday, you'll have to stop hitting the snooze button on your alarm clock and actually wake up as planned. And when you do, you'll realize how liberated and in control you feel. The peace and happiness you're likely to get from that experience will be worth every effort you make from now.

It Solved My Problems with Time Overnight

If there is one quality that distinguishes a high performer from an average one, it is their ability to successfully breeze through a wide range of tasks with high levels of precision, clarity and ease. It is almost as if they are born to multitask and function at elevated levels of effectiveness and efficiency.

Well, they are NOT, and therefore have to cultivate the habit to perform and function as they do. But they all have one thing in common and it is their ability to utilize time when others struggle to have enough of it. Having poured through the success stories of several high performers, I can tell you that they mostly do so by starting early and including a morning routine in their busy schedules.

I Speak from Personal Experience

Incorporating an early morning routine, which gives me an hour of lead time has radically changed the way I complete everything scheduled in a day. The hour I get in the morning helps me indulge in the little things I love (such as enjoying a cup of hot chocolate while reading a book or making something special for my family to have when I'm away). It's also helped me re-asses my priorities better, whether it be within a day and in life in general. I feel happier and therefore am able to go through the rest of the day without any sense of deprivation, guilt or conflict. I'm able to focus better, and have become more time-efficient and productive.

You see, it's the little things we do, with intention, day in and day out, that will eventually make us what we become. And creating an effective morning routine is one of the best ways to start your day with intention. Each morning, you have with you, the window of opportunity to start afresh and do it right. Having a successful morning routine can make the difference between making your mark and falling short of it. Make it count.

Chapter 3 - Sleep Environment

Humans aren't sleeping as nature intended. Years of sociological evolution has distorted the average duration and quality of sleep, not to mention the prevalence of nightmares. Sadly, modernization has comprehensively distorted the very structure and purpose of sleep. This chapter is an attempt to put things into perspective.

Sleep, they say, is the third pillar of good health. The other two are diet and exercise. Being someone who's equally obsessed about all three, I can tell you that sleep is a little more than just a pillar. It's the foundation on which everything else rests. Take it away from the equation and you've got yourself a depleted, deprived, and dejected body (not to forget the host of physical and mental illnesses that come with it). Sleep is crucial for existence which is why this chapter is all about setting a congenial environment that works at getting you plenty of it.

Shifting Your Focus to Your Environment

You are usually a reflection of your surroundings. So when you create a room that makes you happy and at home, you create a space that subconsciously reminds you that:

You are worthy

You are happy

You are confident

You are complete

Your goals are within your reach

You are living your best life

Spending time at creating a pleasant setting in your bedroom can be similar to the experience at a luxurious health resort. You'll feel more relaxed and rejuvenated. You'll look forward to spending your best hours in it. You'll also wake up with the best feeling and that's a great way to start your mornings.

"Do you do anything before bed to make your morning easier?

The kitchen is always cleaned and the house tidied before we go to bed. It's hard work but it's rewarding to wake up to a clean environment. I feel like I start on a fresh note and with a clean slate.

How soon after waking up do you have breakfast?
I eat breakfast soon after my workout and it's been the same way for over 11 years now." - Caroline Reif- Artist and freelance photographer

Making Your Bed. Every Day

Your bedroom is your sanctuary. Now because you spend nearly a third of your life in your bedroom and a good sleep environment is essential for good sleep, it makes sense that you take a moment to focus on everything that makes up this space.

Making your bed as well as tidying your bedroom can reinstate a sense of self-efficacy. You'll feel emboldened to make decisions and live your dreams. Whether those decisions are inside your bedroom or outside of it you'll feel empowered.

If you respect your bed, it will respect you. Think of your bed as a sacred healing space. I know it's tempting to throw things on the bed, it's extra space, right? Don't pile things on it, and if you do, clean it off as soon as you're done with whatever task you were doing. During my school days, I would have stacks of papers and books underneath my pillow, ready to poke me in the face and initiate a stress signal within my body as soon as I woke up. If you are going to put things on your bed, make sure they are things that bring you joy and healing. And limit it to one or two things.

You see, little things such as making your bed every morning puts you in the right headspace. There is also the bonus of returning to a nice-looking bed in the night. A clean, cool, dark and comfortable setting is crucial to create an ideal sleep environment. It really helps to pay attention.

Creating a Technology and Screen-Free Bedroom

If someone paid you every time you saw a person engrossed with his/her cell phone, then you'd be rich by now. Actually, make that super rich!

It's so sad. We claim we've had a night's sleep (and I'm not going into the good or bad of it), but we look beyond tired every morning. Almost all of us, every single morning. Why? More importantly, what then, is disrupting our rest patterns at night?

Just as I type out that question, the culprit stares cheekily at me. Modern light and by that, I mean electric and artificial light coming from cell phones and the likes of pads and laptops have totally distorted the way humans go to sleep.

We discussed before how your biological clock prepares for sleep by increasing the levels of melatonin (responsible for good sleep) in the body. Now for this to happen, your biological clock should first recognize that it is time to sleep. Artificial lighting confuses your suprachiasmatic nucleus into believing the sun has not set yet. That it isn't time to sleep yet. As a result, sleep is delayed, and you lie on your bed scrolling through the digital pages or channels on your screen of choice.

This type of light is everywhere (quite literally) and finding ways to limit exposure to it can be challenging to say the least. Fortunately, it isn't impossible.

- If you have minimal levels of self-discipline, start by keeping your cell phones out of reach. Charge them in another room if you have to.

- Next, create lowered and dim lighting in the room you want to spend your late evenings in. Good mood lighting helps.
- If you have a street lamp outside your bedroom window, installing black-out curtains, work well to maintain complete darkness at night.
- Finally, because blue LED light is common in all technology-driven lights and because the light supresses melatonin and makes it hard to sleep, install software that progressively disperses the harmful blue LED light on your devices. There are apps that will turn on in the evening to filter the blue light.

Staring at a bright screen before bed is a sure way to ensure you won't get to sleep at your desired sleep time. I took the TV out of my bedroom as I realised it had no place in my sacred space. I have an app that filters phone screens into an orange tint. My eyes feel less strained and I no longer have that light phantom shadow behind my eyelids when I close my eyes.

The Alarming Effect

Most of us want to wake up earlier than usual. We want to start the day on a calm and positive note as opposed to a rushed and chaotic one. We want to catch the sun just as it rises and want to spend the first few minutes tucking into our favourite place doing our favourite thing. Sadly, all this mostly translates to wishful thinking for many.

We want to, but we can't...

Because we went to bed, but couldn't sleep

Because we had daily reads to pour through

Because we're so tired and defeated and would love to go back to sleep when we eventually wake up...

This wishful desire to start early and the subsequent inability to wake up as desired, forces us to hold onto external dependants, anything that promises to help us get the job done. This thing we call the alarm clock. It's punctual, it's loud, and it'll rattle you enough to get you out and about in time. Works like magic they say.

Fortunately, I've moved beyond the dependencies of the alarm. If alarming my heart, quite factually, and with it my peace of mind, wasn't terrifying enough, using the snooze feature meant that I was inviting that painful experience over and over again, right at the start of the day. This self-inflicted anxiety stayed with me for the entire day and so I quickly trained my mind (or my mind trained itself) to wake up by itself.

Come to think of it, it wasn't that tough actually. If you can wake up at the same time, every day, irrespective of whether it is the weekend or holiday for a period of a month, (and you can use the help of an alarm while you do so for this period) you'll be able to do it without the alarm at the end of the last week. It worked for me and I'm sure it will work for you. However, if you intend to use the alarm, then I recommend you do away with the snooze function. That way you spare your heart and your nerves the repeated shock.

A lot of people have thrown out their table alarm clocks in favour of the alarm clock on their phones. Use it to work in your favour. Instead of setting an alarm with a horrid hair-raising beep tone, download spa or meditation music. Set your alarm with something peaceful to gently coaxed you out of sleep, setting the tone for a lovely day ahead. In retrospect, I suspect a lot of my dislike of waking up was due to the way I woke up; to an annoying, irritating sound. I woke up with negative inner chatter and possibly an intense spike of stress hormones. It doesn't make sense for you to wake up like that and expect to have a great day.

I would also suggest placing your alarm further than an arm's reach of your bed. Instead of hitting the snooze button, you will have no choice but to get out of bed, to shut the alarm off. This will lessen the chance of you sleeping in and taking extra snooze naps.

You Decide Whether or Not You Sleep

As explained in this chapter, your sleep solutions need not be complicated. In fact, most are simple and inexpensive, and the benefits are immediate and so worth the efforts. They can offer you the life-transforming changes you crave for in your life. So go for it.

Chapter 4 - Wake Up Your Body

The average adult spends a little over four hours of screen time in a day. And for some people, it could be 7 or 8 and even more hours. They start their day by checking their phones, then turning on the television. And while that is running in the background, they go about tackling their morning tasks. They drink coffee, have their breakfast, read stuff, feed their pet, and even possibly shower and get dressed with the television blaring in the background. All that background noise must really make it hard to focus and truly experience anything.

You Can Do Better. Your Body Deserves Better

Every night, you spend a good amount of hours in a horizontal orientation, with little movement. Naturally, your body is likely to feel cramped and lethargic. The last thing it needs is to be is jolted into action. Going through any routines right after you wake up without actually preparing your body to fully wake up is one thing, but going through them with noise blazing from your television sets and/or cell phones is another. Imagine the shock and trauma your body is put through- every single morning. I call this aura pollution. You spent the night peacefully recharging. Your body and energetic fields have gone through a period of healing. Give your body and mind the respect it deserves.

Fortunately, there's a way to turn things around. My experience has taught me that a little calm every morning can help you focus better throughout the day. Likewise, a little gentle physical activity right after you wake up can play the perfect set-up for an eventful day ahead. Starting your day with any form of gentle physical activity can be a great way to cut back on the background noise and be alone with your thoughts. Ask me and I'll tell you that it can be your best mood booster.

Let Your Body Come Alive

Physical fitness plays a key role in helping you feel, look, and be your best all day. It is its own reward. Not only do you feel good when you exercise, but you also carry that wonderful feeling for the rest of the day. And what best way to dedicate the best part of your day (your mornings) to this life-transforming routine?

Get Started First Thing

Get stretching! Starting your day with as little stretch session and later with a simple workout routine can do wonders to your body and mood. Your brain releases endorphins and you feel inspired and excited to breeze through whatever comes your way. When you engage in a physical activity earlier on in the morning, you trigger hyper-oxygenated blood into your frontal cortex, the part of your brain that you use for reasoning, thinking, and decision making. And so, you end up feeling wide awake and alive for several hours afterward. It is, in my opinion, the best gift that you can gift yourself.

My Morning Routine Makes My Body Feel Alive and Ready

I exercise three times a week and I do it in the mornings. I swear by this fitness ritual and sometimes am willing to move mountains to fit it in my schedule. While I might be willing to compromise on other routines, with this one, I simply don't budge.

Although I admit that it wasn't easy at first, I've learned of ways to work around my morning laziness. I trick myself into waking up early and exercising by placing my gym bag right next to my bedroom door. That way, I have them staring at me when I open my bedroom door, like a pet that needs to be fed. And before I even realize it, I find myself beaming and half way into my workout routine.

Start Today

You can, right now, make a decision that'll alter the trajectory of your life and I mean it in the best way possible.

Include a fitness-driven morning routine of some kind and follow it religiously for at least a week (because that's all it will take for you to begin seeing results). Challenge yourself to follow on your decision. Likewise, reward yourself when you achieve a milestone. This will keep you motivated to go after the next milestone and the next and the next. And before you know it, it will be a part of your life. You no longer will have to work at it. That's when you'll feel your most liberated self and that feeling is worth every effort you make from now. Take my word for it.

Your Morning Routine Can Unleash Unlimited Potential

It takes a lot of self-discipline and willpower to stay consistent. And so, when you reach a phase where you're able to stay consistent in your routine, you'll have the willpower and discipline to manifest your dreams to reality. The simple morning you started with would have unleashed your potential to be anything you want to be.

"What is your morning routine?
It varies, but I'll give you the general routine. I wake up about 5:00 A.M. I have a session with my team at 7:00 AM and waking up early gives me the lead I need to be ready to motivate them. I then workout for about an hour. Then it's the usual. I take a shower, have breakfast and head to the gym. But I give everything its time and I do it mindfully so I feel a sense of calm and completion while doing things."- Steve Marshall, Gym Instructor

Start Now. Take the 7 Day Fitness Challenge

- Visualize yourself as your fittest and healthiest self. Now make a decision that you are going to achieve those levels of physical condition in the next few months.
- Include an exercise-driven morning routine that works for you. Keep it simple and realistic to start with. Walking, yoga and stretching come to mind. The key is to start slowly and work up gradually.
- Acquire the tools you need to execute this routine. This could be shifting your other schedules to later or seeking the help of your partner or family to cover for you.
- Be prepared for your toughest mental battle. You're most definitely going to have periods of low. The negative chatter inside your head will do its best to wear you down. But you already know that and that gives you the edge. Stay determined. It won't take long for you to see the benefits such as mental clarity and increased daily stamina.
- Remember that this is your ritual. So stay patient and persistent. Wake up every morning and follow your morning routine

religiously. Transform one morning at a time. Give yourself a few days at least. You'll soon see the benefits.

- Finally, when you have practiced the routine for a week, take a few minutes to calibrate and write down your week's efforts.

How are you feeling?

I assure you that like mine, your experience too will be positive and life-changing.

Chapter 5 - Wake Up Your Mind

Internal Thoughts Lead to External Actions

One could argue that the totality of life is a test to determine the strength and depth of your character. Every event is a lesson that prepares you for that test. The wisdom you gain from study, reflections, as well as life's many lessons will eventually help you develop your character. And while wisdom can be developed inside the sanctity (or sometimes madness) of your mind, your character can only be shaped and tested in relation to your daily life, when you are forced to choose between your personal right and wrong.

It is therefore important that you work on your "inside" just as you work on your "outside." They are equally important and work hand in hand to teach you some of the best lessons in life.

Heading-In Before Heading-Out

The formula to succeed in the outer world is straight forward. You focus, concentrate and work hard at your task, action out your goals and proactively set higher milestones to achieve. The formula to succeed in your inner world is quite the opposite. The universe is always there to guide you. All your questions have an answer. Your problems have a solution. And they all exist within you.

And so, in order to succeed in the inner world, you must not do, you must be. You must let go of all that you've worked so hard to achieve in the outer world. You must let go of the attachment, the sense of pride and achievement as well as the sense of belonging. You must simply surrender to the feelings inside you.

When you detach yourself from everything you passionately hold onto in the outer world, you free your mind from all the noise, the expectations, the disappointments, as well as everything that is in between. Only then will you be able to live in the present and receive answers to your questions.

While the second part of this book addresses ways to succeed in the inner world (where I share morning routines with meditation scripts that will also be available in audio format), this chapter focuses on ways to tap into your inner mojo.

Starting Your Day with a Meditation Routine

Meditation can take many forms and can mean different things to different people. To some, it can be a vacation or a way of escape from the chaotic reality that surrounds them or a way to calm their mind and transcend it to a state of fewer thoughts and conflicts. To others, it can be a gateway to an alternate state of being or awareness, a state where they can manifest all that they wish to be. Some simply don't understand it and see it as a waste of time.

In order to understand its relevance and meaning in your life, you must first practice it with openness and surrender (even if the mere idea of sitting down to meditate every morning does not appeal to you right now). You must let go of any pre-conceived notions or expectations. Only then will you be able to experience moments of mindfulness, greater energy, focus, and calm. It's hard work alright, but once you get the hang of it, it becomes as easy as breathing.

What is your morning routine?

"I'm very fortunate to have a home office, so I don't have to travel much. I wake up without an

alarm on most days, often just before the sunrise.. I then find a quiet place (typically the same corner in my living space) and meditate for 30 minutes. I try and focus on my breath and block out other thoughts for the first few minutes. When I'm nearing the end of the meditation, I compose how I'd like my day to flow. I evaluate my tasks and enact how I'd like to do them in mind. I find this gives me preparation to go through the day. Then, I'm hungry as hell and so I have coffee and breakfast together. I make sure I keep my phone and laptop out of sight. I also eat mindfully and finish everything on my plate."- Jemma Watson, Yoga instructor

It Has Transformed My life

Having been introduced to meditation fairly young; I have an enriching and a second-nature relationship with it. Meditation has liberated me in more ways than one. It has helped me realize my potential and manifest my dreams. I have more control over my thoughts and actions. I nurture loving, meaningful and satisfying relationships with my loved ones. I empathise better. I understand gratitude and don't take my success for granted.

Meditation has helped me overcome periods of stress, anxiety, boredom, and ailments. It has shifted many of my weaknesses to strengths, made me feel complete and happy. I've gained immensely from my morning meditation routine and now I cannot wait to share it with you. I'm sure the results will be equally rewarding for you.

The Power of Verbal and Visual Affirmations

Verbal confirmations, also known as affirmations are words you wilfully choose to use, and by that, I mean think, speak, and believe in order to flesh out the reality you seek. Your mind constantly reaches out to power words as a way to reinstate all that it plans to practice. In fact, there're probably several of these "power words" running through your head, just as we speak. "I can, I am well, I am beautiful." These words help endorse positive thoughts and actions.

Now just as verbal confirmations use words to alter negative thoughts and realize dreams, visualization uses graphics, both motion and still, to derive the same effect. Both are equally effective. They simply energize and help recreate all that you think in your mind, which is why it's extremely important to visualize and think positively.

I've gained So Much

Through personal experience, I've witnessed affirmations elevate my life and the meaning I seek from it. As a writer, I often find myself toggling between two conflicting worlds. The inner one needs me to stay thoughtless and still so as to create and manifest. The outer one requires me to communicate and emote so as to interact and fit in. Sometimes, toggling between the two can be a challenge. Affirmations help me step in and out of the creative world quite seamlessly. It helps me connect and disconnect at freewill and that's quite empowering to say the least.

Creating "Meditative Moments" Out of the Ordinary

Meditation is the act of being mindful and is a great way of connecting with your thoughts. While this should come naturally to us, years of social evolution, in some respects has made us function in a backwards manner. Meditation takes many forms and it's entirely up to you to find a routine that works best for you. You can sit in silence for several minutes or find a meditative routine in making breakfast every morning. You can also take up running as a form of movement meditation. There will always be ways to create meditative moments if you're willing to look. Any routine that allows you to escape the world around you, so as to let you peak into the world inside you, is a routine worth habituating to.

Practicing Gratefulness Every Morning

You've heard the adage that describes gratitude as the most powerful attitude. If you've ever experienced gratitude, you would know the authenticity of this statement. When you are grateful, the universe automatically ensures that you attract the right people, places, events and situations that give you more reasons to feel grateful for your life. It's an effortless way to create your desired reality.

Recognize the things you have been freely gifted with in your life - like a reasonably healthy body, an active mind, relationships you cherish, and so on. This will automatically open you up to gratitude and attract positive things into your life.

When you're grateful for all the wonderful things in your life, you're less likely to crumble when problems creep into your life. The feeling of gratitude will help you see the positive side of challenges. And when you're positive, you can make the impossible possible.

Vision Journaling

Take out a pen and a piece of paper, just as we speak, and write down your answers to the questions below:

1. If your work life and profession were as you wanted them to be, what would they look like? What one trait can you develop to fulfil it?
2. If your relationships were as you wanted them to be, what would it look like? Likewise what quality do you need to work on to make it happen?
3. If your health was perfect in every way, how would you feel and look? Again, what do you need to do to get there?
4. If your finances were as you wanted them to be, how would you feel and look? What do you need to do to get there?
5. If your mental health was in an ideal state, how would you feel and what would you be doing? What steps do you need to take to get there?

6. Visualize the best version of yourself; your dream version. What are the core things that are stopping you from being that person?

Don't rush into the answers. Think about each of the questions and answer with clarity. Likewise, don't worry for the moment about how you are going to achieve them. I'll show you how you can create a routine for them in the chapters to come.

Chapter 6 - Loving Self-Grooming

Here's some good news. An increasing number of people are living their best lives today. People are becoming more aware of their potential and more attuned with their bodies and environment. With the insights presented in this book, you now have the opportunity to be one among them. Your number one goal for yourself should be to live as long and well as you possibly can, and that's where a good morning routine can be your guiding force.

Morning routines work at making you more aware of yourself. They give you a sense of control to exercise your freewill and purpose. You re-gain your sense of self, your sense of knowing and understanding, and that can help you make positive and life-transforming decisions every time.

Turning Your Attention to Your Body

The human body is built to repair wear and tear by the process of replication. If you look at our anatomy carefully, you'll notice that by the rule of spares, we have an additional kidney, an additional lung, an additional gonad and even additional teeth as standby. In fact, our entire DNA system functions on the nature of duplication and repair. When the DNA in our cells become damaged under routine conditions, the cells, using a number of DNA repair-systems replicate and replace the worn out ones. Likewise, when a key gene or a cell is damaged, there are always extra copies of the gene or cell to move in and fill up any vacant positions. Your body is wise and can take care of itself. But it needs you to pay attention to it.

Love Thy Body

As sad as this might sound, it's common to equate how you look to how you feel. And so, it's common to equate being slim (actually skinny) with happiness, social media-approved pictures with happiness, contoured features with happiness, a thinner nose (yes even that) with happiness. Sadly, it's never enough. Good isn't enough. Better Isn't enough. Even more isn't enough. And because how you look automatically equates to how you feel, there's always a subconscious push for something you might want to change in your appearance through extreme measures.

This thought process can be harmful and needs to change. Happiness equals happiness and nothing else. It is a state of being. We are born happy and therefore have to work really hard to preserve that feeling. Thank your hands for having the ability to cook tasty meals and create beautiful art. Thank your legs for giving you the mobility to travel around to see loved ones. Thank your eyes for giving you the privilege to witness the beauty of Earth's nature. Be grateful to your body, for it allows you to exist here.

Change Your Inner Narrative. Treat Yourself the Way You'd Treat Someone You Love

I stopped speaking to myself in a way that I wouldn't speak to my loved ones. If you cannot say it to your children, parents, spouse, siblings, and friends, then you cannot and should not say it to yourself. Likewise, tell yourself the things you tell your loved ones. How about "I love you, I care about you, I need you, and you are doing great?" I do it all the time and it works like magic.

Pamper Yourself

Great, so you've now told your body how amazing it is. How much you love it. How about indulging it too? Give your body the things it yearns for. If wearing good clothes and makeup or doing your hair is what you like, then go for it. Wear clothes that fit and that you feel great in. Get that new haircut and colour you've been wanting. Take a bath occasionally, it works wonders for your self-esteem. Prepare it with bath salts, candles and crystals. The patience and preparation a bath requires, signals to your mind that you are worth the effort. Play ambient or classical music whilst your limbs relax and float in the water.

Be Proactive. Be Prepared

Use your evenings to complete any work that might otherwise restrict you from pampering yourself. For instance, set your clothes on a hanger the night before. You'll save time on deciding what to wear to work and can use that time to do the little things you want to do.

Praise Instead of Compare

As Theodore Roosevelt rightly put it, "comparison is the thief of joy." You don't need to compete with anyone. You are unique and therefore incomparable. So don't compare yourself with someone who you think is better off. Try praising them instead. You'll feel a lot better about yourself afterwards and you can use that feeling to channel the best in you.

Purge everything that Reads Negative

Scroll through your social media accounts (because that's where we get most of the feelings of comparison) and purge anything that makes you feel low. Subscribe to informative and uplifting pages instead. So when the time comes for you to pick up your phone, positive messages are at hand.

Use Your Mornings Wisely

If you think you lack time to give your body the attention it needs, then make time. Wake up earlier than usual and create a morning routine that allows you to spend time with your body. There's always a way-out if you are willing to make yourself a priority, and mornings are a great time to start.

Regulate Your Eating Habits

Most often than not, we eat not because we are hungry, but for the fact of nothing better to do. I used to do this quite a bit. I had developed a habit of eating whenever I sat to watch anything. I had to address this behaviour by practicing mindfulness when it came to food. I suggest making a new habit of eating, only when feelings of hunger kick in. When you eat, eat slowly and mindfully.

Utilize your mornings to listen to your body. Is your body telling you its hungry or is your mind fooling you to indulge it with a few treats? My two cents is to always listen to your body because the body never lies.

Exercise and Maintain a Regular Fitness Routine

Eating healthy goes hand in hand with exercising for a healthy lifestyle. Sign up to the closest gym or indulge in a sport of your liking. Sweat out the toxins in your body through exercise and physical activity.

As mentioned previously, stay positive and motivated. Once you are dedicated enough, you'll see the results flowing in. You'll be dropping off the extra pounds while your skin breathes and glows radiantly. You'll also receive a lot of compliments for your newly acquired looks and fitness level. Although I wouldn't suggest solely relying on externals for your sense of validation. Know and believe you are worthy and beautiful, and the rest will effortlessly fall into place.

Relax and Sleep Over Any Stress

The key is to sleep away any aches and get enough rest. Sleep, they say, is the best form of meditation. Ensuring you get a good night's sleep, every single night, will keep you rejuvenated - both physically and emotionally. What's more, in addition to making you feel better, adequate and quality sleep are key essentials for a healthy and fulfilling lifestyle. Good health is one of the ingredients of overall happiness. And you deserve to be happy.

Chapter 7 - Creating your Routine

"Whether the day is for writing, designing, or painting, the consistent practice of a morning routine is the doorway into it all." – Elle Luna, Artist and Author

Mornings are, for obvious reasons, when you're at your most alert and responsive self. (i) You've had a good night's rest (ii) You start afresh and with a clean slate. It is no wonder why most successful people take advantage of this time and get as much productive work out of it.

When you start early and start productive, you train your brain to follow through on that productivity for the rest of the day. As a result, you end up being less stressed and less reactive. What's more, you get more work done and it almost always turns out better. In essence, having a morning that you can follow and adjust to over time will make successful a tradition for you. This chapter enlists ways to create a morning routine that works for you.

Refer to Your To-Do List

Remember the vision journal I guided you through? Well, now is the time to put it to use. Having a to-do list to refer to and follow will help you stay on track without having to go back and forth on what you might have missed. It's liberating to say the least.

It's the Simplest Way to Increase Your Overall Efficiency

You'll know exactly what you have to do and with a little prep-time the night before, you can actually lay everything out so as to help you stay on point and on top of your routine every morning. I mostly know my morning routine, but still refer to my notes every now and then to ensure I don't miss anything. It helps me focus on the more important things without distraction.

Start Earlier Than Usual

Let's face it; we've all had days when we've felt rushed and exhausted. And if you look back carefully you'll realize that, most often than not, you started your day that way. On the contrary, you most likely achieved more when you started early.

When you start your day early and start your day with the things that matter to you the most, you know that regardless of anything else that happens (or doesn't happen) throughout your day, you got what matters most done. And that's a great feeling to go to sleep with.

Get Real. Start Small

While you might want to start with a bang and plan your morning routine a few hours ahead, without actually easing yourself into a routine, it's possible that you might not be able to follow through with your plan for long. Instead, start small. Begin by waking up 15 minutes earlier, then 30 minutes or 1 hour earlier than your usual time, and follow on this practice for two whole weeks without fail. A good tip is to go to bed 30 minutes to 1 hour earlier than your usual time. Do this for two weeks or until the new schedule becomes doable. On an average, it takes a minimum of fourteen days to cultivate a new habit and about two months to see the benefits from it. Stay the course for this period and you are sure to reap the benefits.

Likewise, break down big goals into smaller ones. You can't dive headfirst into something that's new, big and tough at the same time. There's too much happening there and so you need to habituate to the routine one step at a time.

The slower you take things, the more time you have to observe your response to it and the more likely you are to stay on the routine. Trust me, the smaller the tasks are, the easier to get started on and work through to completion.

Build On Your Routine-One Small Habit at a Time

Choose one new habit at a time to introduce and put all your energy into making that activity a habit before you try something else. You see, the point I'm trying to make here is that you need to take things nice and slow; at a pace that makes you look forward to the next morning.

You can only do something over and over again when you want to do it, when you like to do it, and when you feel your best doing it. Forcing yourself to do several new things at once will only break you down. Instead, only implement one morning tip at a time, one change every fourteen days again. You can always build upon the habit as you progress.

Hold on to Your Will Power

Turning a desire into a ritual requires a lot of long-drawn discipline. Now, the first few days might be easier for many simply because they are most motivated during the initial period. It is usually during the 7th day mark that your enthusiasm tends to wane. That's the time when your body is likely to be adjusting to the changes and your mind begins to feel threatened or less in control. That's when all the doubts, the questions and the reasons for procrastination steps in. Brace yourself and hang in there for another week or so and you'll see the results creep in.

Monitor Your Energy

Developing a new habit takes time and effort and mastering an entire morning routine requires even more of that time and effort. Be prepared. Be happy. Make sure you do the basics right; eat right, eat enough and take a rest when your body asks for it. Remember, your body knows best. So always listen to it.

Stay Open. Stay Updated

Life changes and so do your requirements. Adapt to the need of the hour and be open to make changes to your routine. Improvise and build on them when you think they need some tweaking. Sure, that would mean that you might have to start afresh and start again, but if you've done it once and done it right, you'll have no trouble in doing it again.

Morning Formulas

Based on the results of your Sleep Chart, add these tools (found in Part 2 & Audiobook) and suggestions to your unique morning routine.

HIGH 'REST SCORE' > *Work day Shower Meditation # 1* > Physical Activity

LOW 'REST SCORE' > Light stretching> *Beauty Routine Affirmations* > *Mindful Eating*

HIGH 'DIFFICULTY SLEEPING' > *Weekend Meditation* > Physical activity > *Mindful Commute*

HIGH 'MORNING MOOD' > *Work day shower Mediation #1* > *Beauty Routine Affirmations*

LOW 'MORNING MOOD' > *'Feeling Low' Shower Meditation # 2* or have a bath > Physical Activity > *Mindful Commute*

HIGH 'DAY TIREDNESS' > Light Stretching > Physical activity > *Mindful Eating*

Your Morning Routine

_____

_____

_____

_____

Chapter 8 - Extending your Routine to the Rest of the Household

Once you've mastered the concepts presented in this book, your ability to deal with your own challenges will become a thing of the past. What used to be difficult will become easy. At this point, I ask you to re-direct some of the energies from concentrating mostly on yourself to improving what's happening in your family, and in time, your community. Because what you make of yourself and your family will eventually influence your immediate community and the world at large. It is all tied and every bit matters. This chapter is about preparing you for that incredible eventuality.

Lead By Example

"You must teach men at the school of example, for they will learn at no other." - Albert Schweitzer

Perhaps, the most powerful influence you have on your family, your children in particular, is the example you create in yourself for them to observe all through their years. Your children are always watching and observing you out of the corner of their eyes. They take everything in. And so, irrespective of whether they want to or not, whether they consciously make an attempt or not, your children are inevitably going to pick up some of your traits. Sooner or later, they will begin to emulate your actions. Make it count.

As a kid, I don't remember my parents telling me not to scream. But I remember that they always spoke to me in a gentle and controlled tone-even when they weren't particularly happy with something I did. I learned to speak calmly through observation.

Ask yourself "What human traits are most important to me? What are the qualities I want my family and children to have? What kind of a family would my family be if everyone in it were just like me?"

Create a Routine that Works Around Your Kids, Even With Your Kids

"It's important to note that the morning routines of parents are radically different than those of people without kids."- Dave Asprey, Creator of Bulletproof Coffee

If you have children, like a number of my close friends, then you know what Dave is talking about. Creating morning routines and actually following them can be a daunting task when you have children. Fortunately, there's a way out. Morning routines can be fun and enjoyable when you create them to work with your kids and around their priorities.

You Can't Save Time. You Can Only Spend It Differently

Kids need our time. And as parents, we want to give them our time. We want to spend more time showing them our love just as we want to spend more time nurturing them, taking care of their needs and guiding them. We want to always be there for them, especially at times when they need us the most. But time is something that most people think they lack. They lack the time to do the things that are most important to them. Good news is that you can always make time and better news is that you'll have more of it from today (when you begin to implement the tips presented in this chapter).

Wake Up Before Your Kids

The best way to make some time for yourself is to wake up before your kids wake up. Don't let their wake-up time be your wake-up time. Waking up an hour or so earlier can let you have some uninterrupted time with yourself (when you work on things that matter to your personal growth). Allowing yourself this time will make it easier for you to give them your complete attention when they are awake.

Assess. Adapt. Adopt

Life with children is all about adaptation. As a parent, you want to cater to their needs. And as an individual, you'll have personal needs too. The key to do both is to embrace flexibility and negotiate on a routine that works best for all.

For instance, kids thrive on routine. The sooner you introduce them to routines, the easier it will be for you to meet their needs (as well as yours). Involve your partner. Seek guidance and support. Additionally, involve your kids while preparing the routine if they are old enough to voice their preference. Plan as a family and execute as a team. You'll thank yourself when you begin to see the results.

Cell Phones Should Be Low on the Priority List

I know, easier said than done, but if you can resist the temptation and even make it a rule in the house, you'll see the benefits almost instantly. Remember, your children are taking in everything you do. So, if you or your partner start your day with your phones, then they're going to want to do it too.

Instead, spend that time with them. You've always wanted more time with your family. Now you have it, make the most of it. Do the simple things. Greet them with a smile and your undivided attention when they wake up. Enjoy making and eating breakfast as a family. You can have some great conversations during this time. Talk to them about your childhood and how similar or different it is to theirs. Ask them about their interests.

Check on Their Needs and Make Changes Where Necessary

You can tell the value that something has to you by the amount of time you invest in it and the degree to which you are willing to change for it. On a regular basis, ask your loved ones if they're doing okay. Ask them if there's anything you can do for them.

1. Is there anything that I am doing that you would like me to do more of?
2. Is there anything that I am doing that you would like me to do less of?
3. Is there anything that you would like me to start doing that I am not doing today?
4. Is there anything that I am doing that you would like me to stop doing altogether?

You will be amazed at the quality and depth of the answers you receive. Their answers can guide you to modify your behaviour. And the little changes you make to accommodate their needs can help you maintain a happy, loving and harmonious relationship with your partner, children and other family members.

Over to You

Having a morning routine with your family and loved ones is a great way to start the day. Embrace it; it is everything.

"Over a year ago, my wife and I decided we wanted to start on a morning routine that would help us spend family time with our 4-year-old son. In fact, my wife, son and I started on the

routine together and it's been the same ever since. We wake up at 6:00 AM every morning. Get ready and head for a walk. We talk about his day and the things he learned. We discuss his food interests, then if something catches his eye, he stops to ask and we explain. We've made plenty of friends during this time. There's a cat, a few dogs, and a friendly neighbor he calls uncle. It's a big hit at home and we look forward to it every day" - Jacob Mcnabb, Banker and Catherine, Homemaker

Conclusion

"You will never change your life until you change something you do daily. The secret of your success is found in your daily routine." -- *John C. Maxwell*

Change, real change, comes from introspection and action. It doesn't come from quick-fix techniques that promise to do the "job" overnight. It comes from the desire to know more about yourself and your purpose. It comes from the desire to be more, to be the best you can be. It comes from a sense of openness, where you are willing to alter your lens and see the world differently. It comes from a space of selflessness, where you are open to correct and amend your habits so as to create a better world around you. Finally, it comes from a space of surrender, where you put your best efforts forward and trust the process.

This book, if anything, is an attempt to help you gather the tools to become that change. It is centred on building a foundation for having better mornings, and with it, better days and better lives. Just as you finish reading this book, you have within you, right now, the ability to achieve almost any goal that you can set for yourself. Your biggest responsibility to yourself is to utilize this opportunity. Investing time in understanding what you want and how you can use your best hours to achieve it, is the first step in the right direction. It acts as a guiding force. It has a wealth of potential. What you make of it is entirely in your hands.

Every Morning Is a New Beginning

Tomorrow is a new day. It's ok to fail. It's also ok if you struggled to complete your routine today. Take rest and sleep well tonight, knowing that you always have tomorrow to start afresh and try again.

As I conclude this book, I urge you to make the most of this opportunity. I urge you to stay open and without conflict. I urge you to take notes and reflect on something that catches your eye. Copy and experiment with the lessons you learn. Reflect again and make changes where ever necessary. Adjust, adapt and repeat the process. While this can mean that you might have to go over things over and over again, the results are so worth it.

On A Personal Note

The techniques and tips presented in this book have worked wonders for me. They have transformed my life as well as everyone I have shared it with. The results are real and they are life-changing. That said, I cannot deny that I have days when I'm at my lowest and muster very little or no productivity. I personally struggle with much of what I have shared in this book. But the struggles are worthwhile and rewarding. With time, the struggles are also becoming less frequent and shorter.

This Book Is the Result of that Experience

The experience of those struggles and their subsequent consequences has enabled me to be the best I have ever been (and I know I'll only get better with time). They have taught me to love, serve, and pursue more. They have taught me to be thankful for everything that I have. I've had an enriching experience writing this book and hope you have an equally enriching experience reading it.

Best,
Lola

Part 2

'Work Day' Shower Meditation # 1

(13 Minutes)

Good Morning

Welcome to today

Enjoy the state between wakefulness and
sleep

Feel the warmth and comfort of sleep

Then feel the ease of this day's potential

Slowly wrap your arms around your body.

Take a deep breath in

And slowly release the gift of breath back into
the world

Gently squeeze your arms

Thank your body for resting and allowing you to sleep

Slowly walk to the shower

It is time to coax your body awake

Turn on your shower

Let the water run between your fingers

Not to cold, not to hot

FEEL the ease at which the water slips between your fingers

Step in, your back towards the water

FEEL the pressure against your back

Now FEEL the ease at which the water runs

down your back

The tendrils of water curled around your legs

The pool gathering around your feet

Turn to face the water

FEEL the pressure against your chest

Now FEEL the ease at which the water runs

down your body

The tendrils of water curled around your legs

The pool gathering around your feet

Stretch your arms towards the ceiling

Bend your outstretched arms to the left

Bend your upper-body to the left

Feel the tension

Stand upright and feel the ease

Bend your outstretched arms to the right

Bend your upper-body to the right

Feel the tension

Stand upright and feel the ease

Slowly lower your arms. Relief.

It is time to clean your body.

Reach for whatever tools you need

Sponge, soap, brush, shampoo

Begin to gently clean your neck and work your way down

FEEL the care with every stroke

FEEL the care you are receiving

FEEL the lines, curves and bends of your body

It is time to wake your mind

Notice the water washing the lather off your body

It sloughs off the happenings of yesterday and reveals a clean slate

The water is a gift

Notice how it carries away the dirt, doubts and negativity

It spirals around your legs into and down the drain

Back to the earth

Whisper "Renew" three times

Renew

Renew

Renew

You are now a clean slate

Close your eyes

Listen to the water splash on your skin

The water has transformed into a bright light

Feel this light wash over your body

Filling you with joy, energy and optimism

Open your eyes

What are you grateful for?

Hold the thought for however long you need

Allow the gratefulness to fill your body until
you are ready to end your shower

Have a day filled with wonder.

'Feeling Low' Shower Meditation # 2

(20 minutes)

Morning

I know

You'd rather stay in bed

Away from other people, the world and its

problems

I've been there

Your feelings are valid

Take these next moments to relish in the

comfort of your bed

The covers that have kept you warm

throughout the night

And the pillow that cushions your head

Are you thankful for it?

Slowly roll onto your back

Now, imagine a ball of warm white light float

above your chest

Every breath you take, makes it grow bigger

and bigger

Imagine it grow

Imagine its warmth

As soon as it is as large as your bed

Ask it to drop and engulf you and your bed

Ask it to comfort you

Feel the pain ease away

Realize the light is your own light

You are soothing yourself

You are healing yourself

With that in mind and the knowledge of your

light surrounding your body

It is time to get up

Confidently get out of bed

Feel the ease of this day's potential

Slowly wrap your arms around your body.

Take a deep breath in

And slowly release the gift of breath back into

the world

Gently squeeze your arms

Thank your body for resting and allowing you

to sleep

Slowly walk to the shower

It is time to coax your body awake

Turn on your shower

Let the water run between your fingers

Not to cold, not to hot

FEEL the ease at which the water slips

between your fingers

Step in, your back towards the water

FEEL the pressure against your back

This is yesterday's troubles

Now FEEL the ease at which the water runs

down your back

The tendrils of water curled around your legs

The pool gathering around your feet

The troubles wash down the drain

Turn to face the incoming water

FEEL the pressure against your chest

This is yesterday's anxiety

Now FEEL the ease at which the water runs down your body

The tendrils of water curled around your legs

The pool gathering around your feet

The anxiety washes down the drain

Stretch your arms towards the ceiling

Bend your outstretched arms to the left

Bend your upper-body to the left

Feel the tension

Stand upright and feel the ease

Bend your outstretched arms to the right

Bend your upper-body to the right

Feel the tension

Stand upright and feel the ease

Slowly lower your arms. Relief.

It is time to clean your body.

Reach for whatever tools you need

Sponge, soap, brush, shampoo

Begin to gently clean your neck and work your
way down

FEEL the care with every stroke

FEEL the care you are receiving

FEEL the lines, curves and bends of your body

It is time to wake your mind

Notice the water washing the lather off your
body

It sloughs off the happenings of yesterday and
reveals a clean slate

The water is a gift

Notice how it carries away the dirt, doubts
and negativity

It spirals around your legs into and down the
drain

Back to the earth

Whisper "Renew" three times

Renew

Renew

Renew

You are now a clean slate

Close your eyes

Listen to the water splash on your skin

The water has transformed into a bright light

Feel this light wash over your body

Filling you with joy, energy and optimism

Open your eyes

What are you grateful for?

Hold the thought for however long you need

Allow the gratefulness to fill your body until
you are ready to end your shower

Remember the light that surrounds you

Have a day filled with comfort.

Self-Grooming/Beauty Routine

Affirmations (10 Minutes)

Hello beautiful

Let a smile creep up on your face

It is time to show yourself some love

As you go through your beauty routine

Repeat these affirmations after me:

I am worthy of my love

I am of great value

I am precious

I have beautiful skin

I have wonderous eyes

I have charming lips

I have gorgeous hair

I am well-formed

I am admirable

I am worthy of my love

My face is radiant

My hair is resplendent

My neck is graceful

My nose is shapely

My shoulders are handsome

My hands are divine

My legs are statuesque

My feet are ideal

My body is wonderful

My aura is delightful

I am worthy of my love

I am of great value

I am precious

I have beautiful skin

I have wonderous eyes

I have charming lips

I have gorgeous hair

I am well-formed

I am admirable

My mouth speaks life

My ears hear beauty

My face pleases

My arms comfort

My hands create

My feet lead

My legs form confidence

My eyes show love

My chest protects my heart

I am worthy of my love

My face is radiant

My hair is resplendent

My neck is graceful

My nose is shapely

My shoulders are handsome

My hands are divine

My legs are statuesque

My feet are ideal

My body is wonderful

My aura is delightful

I am worthy of my love

I am of great value

I am precious

I have beautiful skin

I have wonderous eyes

I have charming lips

I have gorgeous hair

I am well-formed

I am admirable

I am beautiful

I am beautiful

Of course I am beautiful

Weekend Morning Meditation

(30 Minutes)

Good Morning

Start by taking a comfortable position

Seated or lying down

Take a deep breath in

And exhale out

Today is a completely new day

A day with new potential

New joys and new laughter

Withdraw your attention from your

surroundings

You are about to journey into a very special
place

Close your eyes

Notice the darkness behind your eyelids

In your mind's eye begin walking forward

Watch as a faint light draws closer and closer

With each step, know you are walking towards
a sacred place

Feel the warmth of the light as you draw near

The light now appears as a line of vertical
light

Keep walking

You now notice it is light piercing through a set of double doors

As you draw closer to the doors you reach your arms out

Push the doors open into an area of bright light

Your eyes adjust and a beautiful garden takes form

Your feet rest on a shiny cobble stone pathway

This leads into a maze of low-lying greenery

Which circles round and round

Until it stops at a magnificent fruit tree

This is your sacred hideout

Your ears pick up on the sound of chirping birds

The gentle rustle of leaves

The splashes of running shallow water

You inhale the sharp scent of wild shrubbery

The tree in the centre intrigues you

It calls out to you

You take your first steps towards the maze

Tucked between the cobble stones are tiny sparkling crystals

They change colour with every step you take

A water fountain archway welcomes you into the maze

You feel the mist cool your skin

As you enter the first ring

You notice the path is lined with a stream on both sides

Dozens of golden fish weave between stalks of water plants

Notice how unbothered they are as they swim deeper and deeper into the maze

You follow their lead around the ring

You feel more relaxed as you journey deeper and deeper.

The entrance to the second ring looms ahead

An arched trellis with vines and bright flowers

You step through the perfumed arch

Into a ring lined with tall flowers

You notice, blue, red, yellow, white, pink flowers

Their heads turn in your direction as you walk

As if you are the sun

They respect, revere and care for you

This is your sacred place

Your well-being is the number one priority

You notice a few flower buds burst open as
you walk by

The flowery aroma is switched out with sweet
tones

You are nearing the third arch way

Your hands brush over an arch coated with
red berries

The last ring is lined with waist length shrubs

Short, deep green and thick, the leaves glisten
as you walk by

The colours of the berries look unearthly

Bright blue hues, deep yellows and translucent reds

Sweet, tangy, spicy aromas linger in the air

It triggers mild hunger

The thought of plucking a sweet succulent berry flits across your mind

It slows your pace for a while

However, you press on

The last arch way eases into sight

It is fashioned with dozens of branches, twigs and roots

Sturdy and ancient, as if nothing could ever destroy it

You are surprised by the gust of wind as you step into the centre of the maze

Flower petals and leaves flit about in the wind

Circling the magnificent tree in the centre

Its roots weave above and below ground

Between pools of fresh water, beds of flowers and groups of shrubs

The cobble stone path way you traversed now divides into a dozen

A lattice of paths lay before you

Let go of the last of your inhibitions

Trust what is within you to guide you

Now make your way to the tree

Are you getting closer?

You know this tree

It has been there your entire life

You sense this the closer you get

You can trust it

It was created for you

This deep knowing settles in, as you reach an
outstretched branch and stop

It's leaves rustle above your head

Every sense of unease has washed away

Peace, that is all you feel in this moment

You tilt your head up and notice a tiny bud

Fixate your attention on this bud

Take a deep breath in

Now breathe in to this bud

Notice how it grows slightly, a fruit peeks out

I have a question for you:

What would you feel like if you had the best
day you could ever have?

Imbed that feeling in your body, feel it grow within you

Now harness the wind around you

Breathe in as much as you can

Now slowly breathe out into the bud

Watch it grow, what colour is this fruit?

Next imagine the events of an idyllic day

Now harness the wind around you

Breathe in as much as you can

Now slowly breathe out into the fruit

Watch it grow bigger and bigger

Next imagine your ideal form of productivity

Your focus, drive, ingenuity

Let it form a feeling of accomplishment within you

Now harness the wind around you

Breathe in as much as you can

Now slowly breathe out into the fruit

The fruit is almost fully formed, bending the branch towards you

Now imagine the best version of yourself

Confident, loving, healthy and important

Let it form a feeling of purpose within you

Now harness the wind around you

Breathe in as much as you can

Now slowly breathe out into the fruit

Watch the fruit grow bigger and bigger

It snaps off and you quickly catch it as it drops

What does your fruit feel like?

Do you need to peel it?

What does it smell like?

Take a bite of your sacred fruit

What does it taste like?

Notice the energy that fills you as you finish your fruit

Thank the tree for providing energetic nourishment

It is time to journey home

Trace your way back to the woody central arch

Notice the vigour in your steps as you make your way back into the third ring

The colourful berries

Red, yellow, blue

The third arch way of red berries

With each step your optimism grows

The flower heads bend in your direction once
again

The second arch way of flowers

The golden fish leap in and out of the stream

A goodbye and good luck

Finally, the first arch

The mist from the water arch tickles your skin

As you make your way to the doors

Make sure to acknowledge your sacred
hideout

Thank it for being a place of refuge and

replenishment

Push through the door

Notice the darkness behind your eyelids

Welcome back

Wiggle your toes

Wiggle your fingers

Stretch your torso

Open your eyes

Take some time to readjust from your journey

It is now time to paint your environment with

the energetic nourishment of your fruit

Stand up

Notice the love within you

Lift your arms up and sway them from side to side

Paint your ceiling with love

Notice the abundance within you

Paint the walls to your right and your back with abundance

Notice the effectiveness within you

Paint the walls to your left and your front with productivity

Notice the wealth of confidence within you

Now walk around your environment

Share your self-esteem with every step

If possible, make your way to an area with
direct sunlight and sit

Otherwise sit in a place you will not be
interrupted

Allow the sunrays to feed you warmth and
light

Like the tree in your sacred hideout

Notice the movement of the Earth you sit on

As it circles around the sun

As it makes its way along its orbital ring

beneath billions of stars

Remember your sacred tree is a constant

Reliable and constant like the sun

Therefore, you are being taken care of

Always and forever

Good morning and have a great day.

Mindful Eating (10 Minutes)

Take a moment to be thankful for the food before you

Acknowledge its service

Its role in your survival

For the next few minutes become intensely aware of the act of eating

Enjoy your meal

Become aware of the colours before you

Become aware of moisture

Become aware of flavours

Become aware of texture

Become aware of aroma

Become aware of your chewing

Become aware of pauses

Become aware of sounds

Become aware of replenishment

Mindful Commute (22 Minutes)

Work commutes are often filled with negative, pessimistic thoughts. Whether it be the traffic, road closures, other drivers or the dislike of your job, these are no reasons to fill your mind with counterproductive thoughts. Let us work together to train your mind and clean up the mind chatter. Every minute you will hear a sensory signal. The goal is to maintain a state of intense alertness until the next signal. No mind chatter or worrying, just pure present moment awareness. Can you do it? Let's find out.

Become aware of light

Become aware of your movement

Become aware of speed

Become aware of stillness

Become aware of darkness

Become aware of transparency

Become aware of your physical control

Become aware of scent

Become aware of liquid

Become aware of nature

Become aware of structure

Become aware of gravity

Become aware of air

Become aware of sound

Become aware of the small

Become aware of shininess

Become aware of dullness

Become aware of the large

Become aware of direction

Become aware of change

Have a good productive work day.

Rainy days, bad habits and

Gatekeepers... follow me as I write my

way to a better life.

www.lolarmarie.com

Made in the USA
Middletown, DE
30 March 2019